My Boyfriend's Back!
The Story of the Girl Groups

The Life, Times, & Music™ Series

My Boyfriend's Back!

The Story of the Girl Groups

The Life, Times, & Music™ Series

Anna Hunt Graves

FRIEDMAN/FAIRFAX
PUBLISHERS

Acknowledgments

Thanks to Ben Boyington, a truly fabulous editor and friend

A FRIEDMAN/FAIRFAX BOOK

© 1995 Michael Friedman Publishing Group, Inc.

ISBN 1-56799-185-8

Editor: Benjamin Boyington
Art Director: Jeff Batzli
Designer: Susan E. Livingston
Photography Editor: Jennifer Crowe McMichael
Production Manager: Jeanne E. Hutter

Grateful acknowledgment is given to authors, publishers, and photographers for permission to reprint material. Every effort has been made to determine copyright owners of photographs and illustrations. In the case of any omissions, the publishers will be pleased to make suitable acknowledgments in future editions.

For bulk purchases and special sales, please contact:
Friedman/Fairfax Publishers
Attention: Sales Department
15 West 26th Street
New York, New York 10010
(212) 685-6610 FAX (212) 685-1307

Website: http://www.metrobooks.com

Printed in Hong Kong by Midas Printing Limited

Contents

Introduction 6

Setting the Stage 11

Female Vocal Groups of the 1950s 14

Girl Groups Storm the Charts 22

The Tycoon of Teen 38

The Motown Sound 52

Say Goodbye to Girl Groups 65

Girl Groups in the 1990s 68

Bibliography 70

Suggested Reading 70

Suggested Listening 70

Index 71

I knew I was going to sing....
I was going to sing, and I was
going to sing rock and roll.

—Ronnie Spector

Introduction

I n the late 1950s, a number of female vocal groups began to produce songs that mixed doo-wop harmonies with rhythm and blues (R&B) music. The groups were usually trios or quartets in which one vocalist sang a lead part while the others contributed background vocals. This arrangement became known as the "girl group" sound, and it flourished during the early 1960s. Girl groups were a constant presence on the Billboard pop charts in 1962 and 1963, but by 1965 the popularity of this sound was waning as it became eclipsed by other musical trends. Although girl groups were successful for only a short time, their sound influenced many of their musical contemporaries, and it continues to have an impact on performers today. The girl group era represents an important part of *the history of the early days of rock and roll as well as the history of*

women in popular music. The emergence of girl groups marked a

turning point for women in rock and roll, for it established a specific

style of performing that listeners associated with women.

Girl groups like the Poni-Tails, a trio that came from Cleveland, Ohio, began to appear in the late fifties.

The girl group sound was the result of a collaborative effort that involved producers, songwriters, instrumentalists, and managers, in addition to the women who sang the songs. Each of these persons, particularly the producer, was significant in determining a particular group's success or failure. As rock critic Greil Marcus points out, "The relationship between singer and producer was dependent; almost none of the great lead singers of girl group rock...achieved even minimal success outside of the direction of the producer originally responsible for her."

Some rock music historians would argue that, because of their lack of autonomy, the girl groups were largely interchangeable and would not

The Bobbettes, an R&B group that recorded for Atlantic Records, pose in a recording studio with (standing, left to right) singer Big Joe Turner, musician Sammy Price, and Ahmet Ertegun, who founded Atlantic in 1947.

have succeeded without the guidance of others. This assessment over-looks the fact that the performers who made up the girl groups were generally very young—most were in their teens and early twenties—which put them at a great disadvantage in terms of artistic control. In her history of women in rock, *She's a Rebel*, Gillian G. Gaar notes, "In later interviews with these [girl group] performers, a recurring complaint is the complete lack of involvement, let alone control, they were allowed in decisions affecting their careers." Female artists were rarely taken seriously by those who ran the music industry in the fifties and sixties, and the girl groups were undoubtedly viewed simply as vehicles for hit songs

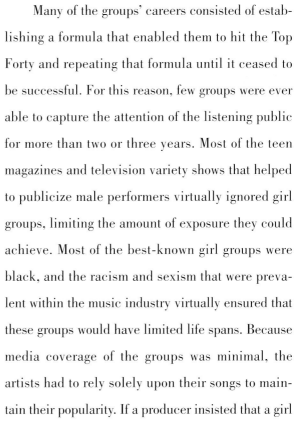

rather than as talented, creative individuals.

Many of the groups' careers consisted of establishing a formula that enabled them to hit the Top Forty and repeating that formula until it ceased to be successful. For this reason, few groups were ever able to capture the attention of the listening public for more than two or three years. Most of the teen magazines and television variety shows that helped to publicize male performers virtually ignored girl groups, limiting the amount of exposure they could achieve. Most of the best-known girl groups were black, and the racism and sexism that were prevalent within the music industry virtually ensured that these groups would have limited life spans. Because media coverage of the groups was minimal, the artists had to rely solely upon their songs to maintain their popularity. If a producer insisted that a girl group record songs resembling the tune that had been their initial success, the public would predictably soon grow tired of the group. And once the public's interest waned, the producer would abandon the group and move on to another project; this abandonment usually signaled the end of the group's career.

Since most groups lacked an image that could be connected with their music, audiences often received little or no information about the individuals who made up a particular group. Girl group artists were generally identified by their group name alone, and the membership of any given group often changed from one record to the next. Producers occasionally used unnamed session or backup vocalists to sing under the name of a successful group, and some groups recorded under more than one name. When the girl group era more or less came to an end in the mid-sixties, most of the artists who were still actively pursuing musical careers faded into obscurity. Although a number of the groups continued to perform in the following decades, often singing in oldies revival shows, their whereabouts today are largely unknown.

While the story of the girl groups is the story of the performers, producers, songwriters, and others who came together to manufacture the girl group sound, it is also a snapshot of a specific time period in which individuals who have for the most part been forgotten helped change the direction of popular music.

The Chords, shown here in a publicity photo, scored a hit with "Sh-Boom," the flip side of their debut single released on Cat Records.

Setting the Stage

In the 1950s, American popular music had arrived at a crossroads, with the emergence of different styles such as rockabilly, rhythm and blues, and doo-wop. These and a variety of other musical forms, including jazz, blues, country, and gospel, became ingredients for a new hybrid genre that emerged early in the decade and soon came to be known as rock and roll. The popular music establishment was reluctant to acknowledge this new sound, and mainstream major labels such as Decca, RCA Victor,

11

Columbia, Mercury, and Capitol Records largely ignored it even as it gained popularity. Their disregard gave independent record companies that had previously specialized in country and western or rhythm and blues an opportunity to take the lead by making records that would create a foundation for rock and roll. These small "indie" labels offered audiences alternatives to the music that was being produced by the majors, and they realized a potential market in white teenagers who were bored with the musical status quo.

Although the Crew Cuts copied the Chords' arrangement of "Sh-Boom" and beat the Chords to the top of the charts, the black group's original version received more airplay than the white group's cover.

45s

Music today can be found in a variety of formats, including compact discs (CDs), CD singles, cassette tapes, cassette singles, digital audio tapes (DATs), and the rapidly vanishing vinyl record album. Columbia Records introduced the 33⅓ rpm long-playing record (LP) in June 1948, and less than a year later, RCA Victor issued the first 45 rpm single. By the mid-1950s, 45s were more popular than 78 rpm records, which had previously been the standard format of the music industry. When the girl group genre began to develop in the late fifties and early sixties, the 45 was the driving force of the popular music industry, outselling all other formats until the late sixties. Generally having only one song on each side, 45s were perfect for jukeboxes, disc jockeys, and listeners who wanted to hear only hit records. Many of the LPs produced by early rock performers consisted of two or three hits (also released on 45s) separated by filler songs. The albums released by most girl groups fell into this category, and as a result the groups are remembered for their singles rather than for their LPs.

Before the advent of rock and roll in the mid-1950s, African-American performers were largely excluded from the realm of popular music. Early in the decade, as white teenagers began to take an interest in rhythm and blues—a genre aimed primarily at black audiences—record companies became aware of the potential for artists to "cross over" from one market to another. By 1954 white pop artists on major record labels were copying songs originally recorded by black artists on independent labels, a practice known as "covering." One of the first major crossover records was an R&B song called "Sh-Boom" recorded on the Cat label (distributed by Atlantic Records) by the Chords, a black male vocal group. When this song entered the pop charts at number sixteen, Mercury Records released a cover by a white male group known as the Crew Cuts, which became even more successful on the charts, eventually reaching the number one spot. This strategy soon came to be used to generate hit songs for white female vocal groups as well.

In addition to recording numerous hit records, the Andrews Sisters appeared in twenty-two films over the course of their career, which lasted from the early 1930s until the mid-1950s.

Female Vocal Groups of the 1950s

In 1937 the Andrews Sisters became the first all-female vocal group to record a song that sold more than a million copies. "Bei Mir Bist Du Schon," a Yiddish tune rewritten in English, introduced American music fans to LaVerne (1915–1967), Maxene (1917–   ), and Patty Andrews (1920–   ), who went on to become superstars for Capitol Records over the next two decades. The success of the Andrews Sisters established a precedent for a number of other "Sister" groups that became popular during the 1950s, including the DeJohn Sisters, the Fontane Sisters, the Lennon Sisters, the DeCastro Sisters, the Shepherd Sisters, and the McGuire Sisters.

This last group, who signed with Coral Records, a subsidiary of Decca formed in 1949 as an R&B label, was the most successful sister group. The McGuire Sisters first hit the charts in July 1954 with "Goodnight, Sweetheart, Goodnight," which had previously been released on the Vee Jay label by a group called the Spaniels (the song had also been a hit for crooner Rudy Vallee in 1931). Their follow-up effort, a song called "Sincerely," which had been recorded by the Moonglows on Chess Records, went to number one in December 1954 and became one of the most popular singles of 1955. While the McGuire Sisters became known for their covers of doo-wop songs, their slickly crafted pop sound bore

The DeCastro Sisters were one of many sister-based vocal groups that made the Top Forty during the mid-fifties.

very little resemblance to rhythm and blues, even though it was derived from that style of music. Although the songs of the McGuire Sisters and other female pop groups of the fifties lacked originality and did not qualify as rock and roll—and these performers are not considered "girl groups" in the sense of the sound that was established in the sixties—these groups certainly played a part in making possible the success of the girl groups that would appear in later years.

Another female vocal group that became popular during the 1950s was the Chordettes, who made a name for themselves with their unique barbershop quartet style. They made their debut on the Cadence label in

Unlike many of the girl groups that followed them, the sister combos of the fifties were usually signed by major record labels. The DeJohn Sisters recorded for Epic Records in the mid-fifties.

The McGuire Sisters

In March 1958, the McGuire Sisters were featured on the cover of *Life* magazine, which pronounced them "the country's top girl vocal group." Born in Middletown, Ohio, Christine (1929–), Dorothy (1930–), and Phyllis McGuire (1931–) were the daughters of a minister, and they began singing together in church at an early age. After appearing on *Arthur Godfrey's Talent Scouts*, a popular television program on which many musical careers were launched, they made the transition to pop music and became regular performers on the show. After releasing two hit singles in 1954, their album *By Request* became one of the top-selling LPs of 1955. Between 1954 and 1960, they produced commercials for Coca-Cola, performed regularly in nightclubs in major cities, and continued to record successfully.

late 1954 with "Mr. Sandman," which became their first and biggest hit, remaining in the Top Ten for sixteen weeks. (This song was subsequently covered by a number of other artists, including a male vocal quartet known as the Four Aces.) The Chordettes are perhaps best known for the song "Lollipop," a novelty tune recorded in early 1958. Later that year, a trio called the Poni-Tails (Toni Cistone, LaVerne Novak, and Patti McCabe), who recorded for the ABC-Paramount label, went to number seven on the charts with "Born Too Late."

At the same time that white groups such as the McGuire Sisters were attracting attention with their well-polished singing styles, black female groups were producing some significant material of their own with a sound

The Chordettes

A quartet originally from Sheboygan, Wisconsin, the Chordettes first attracted national attention in 1949 when they appeared on *Arthur Godfrey's Talent Scouts*. Dorothy Schwartz (lead vocal), Jinny Osborn (tenor), Carol Bushman (baritone), and Janet Ertel (bass) became regular performers on the show during the early fifties, and they developed a successful working relationship with Godfrey's musical director Archie Bleyer. In 1953 Lynn Evans replaced Schwartz as the group's lead vocalist, and the Chordettes left the Godfrey show to record for Bleyer's recently founded Cadence label. The following year, Bleyer married Janet Ertel, and "Mr. Sandman" (recorded with a flight attendant named Margie Needham filling in for Jinny Osborn) went to number one for seven weeks, selling over a million copies.

For the next seven years, Bleyer directed the Chordettes' career, choosing their songs, writing their arrangements, and producing their records. He made a particular effort to appeal to the teenage market by having the group sing R&B-based tunes such as "Eddie My Love" (originally recorded by the Teen Queens in early 1956 and covered again later that year by the Fontane Sisters) and "Charlie Brown" (a 1959 hit for a male group called the Coasters). These R&B records did not seem to work as well for the Chordettes as did their normal repertoire of smooth songs with orchestral backgrounds derived from the pop styles of the 1940s. "Lollipop," a bouncy novelty song submitted to Bleyer by a duo known as Ronald and Ruby, became the group's second million-selling single in 1958. In 1961 the Chordettes had their last Top Twenty hit with "Never on Sunday." While they were never really considered part of the girl group scene because of their fifties sound, they continued to perform during the early sixties as a cabaret act.

that was unquestionably closer to rock and roll. The Bobbettes were signed by Atlantic Records in 1957, and in May of that year they had a hit with "Mr. Lee," a song they had written about their fifth-grade teacher. "Mr. Lee" went to number one on the R&B charts and made it to number six on the pop charts. Although the Bobbettes were never able to repeat the success of this first release, they attempted to revive their career in 1960 with a sequel song entitled "I Shot Mr. Lee," which fizzled at number fifty-two on the pop charts.

The Chantels were another black group that appeared in the late fifties and displayed a more distinctive R&B sound than their white counterparts. Like other black girl groups, they were inspired by male doo-wop artists, particularly Frankie Lymon and the Teenagers, a group best known for such songs as "Why Do Fools Fall in Love" and "I'm Not a Juvenile Delinquent" (both released in 1956). The Chantels began recording for the End label in 1957, and within a year the group had reached number fifteen on the pop charts with "Maybe," a song written by their manager and producer, Richard Barrett. While they went on to record a number of other songs that made it into the Top Forty, the Chantels were unable to sustain their career, partly as a result of tension caused by financial problems. After undergoing

The Bobbettes

Ranging in age from eleven to fifteen years old when they signed their recording contract, the Bobbettes were one of the youngest girl groups to have a hit record. Heather Dixon, Jannie Pought, Emma Pought, Helen Gathers, and Laura Webb were classmates who started singing together at parties in New York during the mid-fifties. After forming a group called the Harlem Queens, which initially had eight members, they began performing at local talent shows, including Amateur Night at the Apollo Theater. In 1957 James Dailey became their manager and helped them get a deal with Atlantic Records. Under Dailey's management, the group changed its name to the Bobbettes and recorded several original compositions, scoring their first and only hit with "Mr. Lee."

The Chantels

Although the Chantels did not come together as a group until 1956, they had been singing with one another in the school choir since the second grade. While attending St. Anthony of Padua School in the Bronx, Sonia Goring (1940–), Lois Harris (1940–), Jackie Landry (1940–), Arlene Smith (1941–), and Rene Minus (1943–) organized a group named after a rival school, St. Francis de Chantelle. After being discovered by Richard Barrett, who had previously performed with a group of his own called the Valentines, the Chantels recorded their first two songs. "He's Gone" and "The Plea" were both written by Smith, the group's lead singer. These two songs were released as a 45 in August 1957, and the record went to number seventy-one, a respectable accomplishment for a group's debut effort.

The Chantels' next single, "Maybe," ultimately proved to be their biggest record, although they also had two other hits in 1958 with "Every Night (I Pray)" and "I Love You So." By this time, however, the girls had realized that they were not making any profit on their recordings, since their earnings were being used to pay for various expenses incurred by their label. The Chantels became disillusioned by this situation, and in 1959 Smith and Harris left the group. Smith went on to record several solo records for different labels in the early sixties, including an unsuccessful remake of the Clovers' 1956 hit "Love, Love, Love," produced by Phil Spector. Meanwhile Barrett found the Chantels a new lead singer, Annette Smith, and they recorded two songs on the Carlton label: "Look in My Eyes" and "Well, I Told You" (both released in 1961). Both tunes made it onto the charts; the first went to number fourteen, the second to number twenty-nine.

personnel changes, the Chantels continued performing and recording into the sixties, although they never managed to repeat the success of "Maybe."

At this time, many people within the record industry began to feel that girl groups could not be consistently successful singing rhythm and blues. This belief often made it difficult for girl groups to attract the attention of a label, and many groups that were signed may not have gotten the promotion they deserved. In addition, the popular music industry in the late fifties continued to be dominated by male singers and groups. In

spite of these obstacles, the early girl groups did have an impact on some listeners, not to mention a few producers and songwriters. Although they were unable to take advantage of the musical trend they helped to create, artists like the Chantels played an important role in providing the fuel for the girl group explosion of the early sixties.

Girl Groups
Storm the Charts

In January 1961, the Shirelles became the first girl group to reach number one on the *Billboard* charts with "Will You Love Me Tomorrow?," a song written by Carole King and Gerry Goffin and recorded on the Scepter label. After Johnny Mathis had turned down the song, the Shirelles' producer, Luther Dixon, heard it and convinced the composers that it was right for a girl group. In 1962 the Shirelles had a second number one song with "Soldier Boy," and several of their subsequent releases made the Top Ten. When Dixon left Scepter to work for Capitol, the Shirelles began to lose their momentum as pop stars. "Foolish Little Girl," released in 1963, was their last successful song, and by that time they were only one of many girl groups that were appearing on the pop charts.

Carole King (1942–   ) and Gerry Goffin (1939–   )

Born Carole Klein in Brooklyn, New York, Carole King is one of the most successful female songwriters in the history of popular music. While she is best known for her 1971 album *Tapestry*, which featured the hit single "It's Too Late/I Feel the Earth Move" and earned her four Grammy Awards, including Record of the Year and Best Female Vocalist, her career actually began more than a decade before this record was released. King learned to play the piano when she was only four years old, and by the time she was a teenager she was composing music for a quartet she created known as the Co-Sines. In 1958 King met Gerry Goffin while they were attending Queens College in New York City. A few years later, they were married and collaborating as songwriters for Aldon, a Manhattan-based music publishing company started in 1958 by Al Nevins and Don Kirshner.

While working for Aldon, Goffin and King helped establish what became known as the Brill Building sound, named after an office building located at 1619 Broadway, in the center of the New York music district (an area in midtown Manhattan that was home to several music publishing companies—the Tin Pan Alley of the fifties and sixties). Although Aldon's office was actually across the street from the Brill Building, the two songwriters became part of the community of composers who created some of the most popular songs of the early 1960s. In addition to the hits recorded by various girl groups, some of Goffin and King's most successful songs include "Take Good Care of My Baby" (1961) by Bobby Vee, "The Loco-Motion" (1962) by Little Eva, "Up on the Roof" (1962) by the Drifters, "I'm Into Something Good" (1964) by Herman's Hermits, and "(You Make Me Feel Like) A Natural Woman" (1967) by Aretha Franklin.

King generally wrote most of the music for their compositions, while Goffin contributed the lyrics.

Although King's talent as a singer did not fully emerge until the early 1970s, she did record several songs during the late fifties on the ABC-Paramount label. Although these songs failed to achieve any recognition, in 1962 she had a hit on the British and American pop charts with "It Might As Well Rain Until September," released on Aldon's Dimension label. By this time she and Goffin had two daughters, Sherry and Louise, and King seemed to be satisfied playing the role of writer, arranger, and producer. In the middle of 1963, Aldon was purchased by Columbia Pictures–Screen Gems, an organization that owned two record labels: Colpix Records and Screen Gems Music. Goffin and King continued to produce songs for these and other labels, but the market for their music was beginning to decrease and they eventually ceased their collaborative efforts. They divorced in 1968 and moved separately to California. At the height of their success in 1962, Carole King and Gerry Goffin hit the Top Forty seventeen times with their compositions, and together they made a substantial contribution to the girl group sound.

The Shirelles

The four young women who eventually came to be known as the Shirelles began singing together while they were still in high school, calling themselves the Poquellos. After Addie "Micki" Harris (1940–1982), Beverly Lee (1941–), Shirley Owens (1941–), and Doris Coley (1942–) won a school talent competition in Passaic, New Jersey, singing a song they had written called "I Met Him on a Sunday," they were signed to a small label called Tiara Records.

The record company was owned by Florence Greenberg, whose daughter Mary Jane attended school with the group and had suggested that they audition for her mother. The girls renamed themselves the Shirelles, and in the spring of 1958 they released "I Met Him on a Sunday." Greenberg leased the song to Decca Records, and the Shirelles' first single made it to number forty-nine on the *Billboard* pop charts.

In 1959 Greenberg created a label called Scepter Records, hiring songwriter and producer Luther Dixon to work with the Shirelles. Their next record, a cover of the Five Royales' song "Dedicated to the One I Love," reached only number eighty-three. However, the Shirelles followed up in 1960 with "Tonight's the Night," a song written by Owens and Dixon that went to number thirty-nine after some competition with the Chiffons, who took their version of the song to number seventy-six.

After this accomplishment, Dixon suggested that the group record "Will You Love Me Tomorrow?" At first the Shirelles protested, saying that the song's demo (performed by songwriter Carole King) sounded too much like a country and western record. When Dixon and King came up with a new musical arrangement, the group agreed to do it. The result was a pop masterpiece, featuring a prominent string section and an up-tempo drumbeat (with King herself playing timpani), that gave the Shirelles (and the songwriting team of Goffin and King) their first number one hit on the pop and R&B charts. A month later, "Dedicated to the One I Love" was reissued and quickly rose to number three.

In the spring of 1961, the Shirelles embarked on a tour of the United States; meanwhile, their next single, "Mama Said," hit

sion in a single take, "Soldier Boy" was originally meant to be a filler song on one of the Shirelles' albums.

The group went on to rack up three more Top Forty singles with Dixon as their producer before he ceased working with them at the end of 1962. During this period, the Shirelles were offered singer Gene Pitney's composition "He's a Rebel" (which the Crystals would later record and make into a number one hit), but Greenberg rejected the song, thinking it might be controversial in the South.

The Shirelles' final Top Ten record, "Foolish Little Girl," appeared in May 1963. By this time, the girl group sound the Shirelles had pioneered had exploded on the charts and competition was fierce. The Shirelles were no longer Scepter's main priority, for Greenberg now had other stars, including Dionne Warwick, who occasionally filled in for members of the Shirelles at live shows and sang backup vocals on some of their songs.

Greenberg was supposed to be holding a large portion of the Shirelles' earnings in a trust fund until they reached the age of twenty-one. When they realized that the money no longer existed, they attempted to dissolve their relationship with Scepter and sign with another label. Because of legal entanglements, however, the Shirelles were unable to sign a new contract, and Scepter continued to release material the group had already recorded.

In early 1965, a song called "Are You Still My Baby?," which barely broke into the Top One Hundred, became the group's last chart entry for two and a half years. The Shirelles were eventually able to record for other labels, including Mercury and Bell Records, but none of their subsequent releases came close to achieving the success of their early recordings.

number four. This was followed by a handful of releases that failed to break into the Top Forty. At the beginning of 1962, songwriter Burt Bacharach offered the group "Baby It's You," a song he had cowritten with his partner, Hal David, and the Shirelles turned it into a Top Ten hit.

A few months later, "Soldier Boy" became the group's third million-selling single. Composed by Luther Dixon and Florence Greenberg and recorded at the end of a ses-

Another group that found its way to stardom with songs written by Goffin and King was the Cookies, who debuted on Dimension Records in late 1962 with "Chains," a song later covered by the Beatles. They had already made the charts unofficially as the backing vocalists on Little Eva's smash "The Loco-Motion," also a Goffin-King composition. "Chains," their first release under their own name, went to number seventeen, and was followed in 1963 by "Don't Say Nothin' Bad About My Baby," which reached number seven. This turned out to be the peak of their career, although they did record several other moderately successful

The Cookies

Like many of the girl groups, the Cookies were discovered in New York. Although founding members Dorothy Jones and Ethel "Earl-Jean" McCree had been born in the South, they both moved to Brooklyn at an early age, where they got together with Margaret Ross to form the Cookies. When they made their performing debut, winning a contest at the Apollo Theater's Amateur Night, they attracted the attention of an Atlantic Records employee who hired them as backup singers for recording sessions. They went on to sing with Neil Sedaka on some of his early recordings for RCA, and at his suggestion they began working with composer Carole King. In July 1961, Jones made a solo recording, "It's Unbearable," written, produced, and arranged by King and her partner, Gerry Goffin, and released by Columbia Records. The song failed to break onto the charts, but the Cookies established a relationship with Goffin and King that would soon lead them into the Top Ten.

songs. The group's lead singer, Earl-Jean, had a brief solo career, with one release, "I'm Into Something Good" (written by Goffin and King), that made the Top Forty in 1964.

In late 1962, a New York group called the Chiffons went into the studio to record "He's So Fine," a quintessential girl group song that described a girl's attraction for a boy. A few months later, after the song had been rejected by Capitol Records, it was released on an independent label called Laurie, which had emerged in the late fifties with hot songs by Dion and the Belmonts. "He's So Fine" went on to become the number

Clockwise from left: Aldon Music founders Don Kirshner and Al Nevins, songwriters Gerry Goffin and Carole King, and Little Eva. Sixteen-year-old Eva Boyd was a babysitter for King and Goffin when she recorded "The Loco-Motion." Goffin recalls that he and King were inspired to write the song after seeing her dance around their house "like a locomotive train."

one song in the country, selling more than a million copies. The Chiffons followed up with "One Fine Day," a Goffin-King tune originally recorded by Little Eva. For this recording, the producers erased Little Eva's vocal and replaced it with the voices of the Chiffons; the result became a Top Ten single. The group's final Top Forty record, "Sweet Talkin' Guy," appeared in 1966.

During the early sixties, as the girl group sound invaded and became a mainstay of the pop charts, a number of groups established them-

The Chiffons

In 1960, Judy Craig (1946–), Sylvia Peterson (1946–), Patricia Bennett (1947–), and Barbara Lee (1947–) came together while attending high school in the South Bronx to form the Chiffons. In the fall of the same year, they had a minor hit on the Big Deal label with "Tonight's the Night" (a song the Shirelles had recorded earlier that year), featuring Craig as lead singer. Ronnie Mack (d. 1963), a local songwriter who became their manager, helped them record demo tapes that eventually got them signed to Laurie Records in 1962. The Chiffons attracted the interest of a production team named Bright Tunes, a group of four men from Brooklyn—Phil Margo, Mitch Margo, Hank Medress, and Jay Siegel—who were better known as the Tokens, a band that had gone to the top of the charts with "The Lion Sleeps Tonight" in 1961.

By early 1963, the Chiffons had established themselves with "He's So Fine," written by Ronnie Mack, who died of Hodgkin's disease a few months after the song became a success. The group's follow-up release, "One Fine Day," which came out a few months after "He's So Fine," went to number five. The Chiffons subsequently recorded several songs for Bright Tunes under the pseudonym the Four Pennies. Although some of these songs made it onto the charts, none of them did as well as the songs credited to the Chiffons. In the summer of 1964, the Chiffons opened up for the Rolling Stones on the latter band's first tour of the United States. Later that year the Chiffons sued Bright Tunes in an effort to free themselves from a contract that allowed their producers to use large portions of the royalties generated by Chiffons songs to pay for studio time. Because the Chiffons had been minors when they signed the original agreement, the court ruled in their favor. However,

as a result of the lawsuit, other labels were reluctant to get involved with the group, and they eventually returned to Laurie, signing directly with the label.

In the middle of 1965, the Chiffons released a song called "Nobody Knows What's Goin' On (In My Mind But Me)," which was a mixture of psychedelic pop and rhythm and blues. This song peaked on the charts at number forty-nine, but a year later the group was back in the Top Ten with "Sweet Talkin' Guy." The Chiffons continued to record and tour through the late sixties, but they never had another hit record. In 1976, they made an effort to revitalize their career with a song called "My Sweet Lord," written by former Beatle George Harrison. The song had sold a million copies when Harrison recorded it in 1970, and Ronnie Mack's estate had sued Harrison a year later because of the tune's resemblance to "He's So Fine." Harrison was found guilty of "subconscious plagiarism" and forced to give part of his earnings from the songs to Mack's inheritors. The Chiffons' attempt to capitalize on the publicity generated by the case failed to attract the public's attention, and they did not profit from the outcome of the trial.

The Angels

Sisters Barbara Allbut and Phyllis "Jiggs" Allbut, both of whom sang in their high school choir in Orange, New Jersey, teamed up with Linda Jansen to form a group called the Starlets. After recording a couple of songs for a local label, the trio was signed by Caprice Records. They renamed themselves the Angels, and in October 1961 had their first hit with "Till," which went to number fourteen. The following year, Jansen was replaced by Peggy Santiglia and the Angels began working with the songwriting and production team of Richard Gottehrer, Bob Feldman, and Jerry Goldstein, who composed "My Boyfriend's Back" specifically for the Angels. When the song was released a few months later, it quickly became a huge hit, and the Angels began touring in support of the record. Their next two singles, "I Adore Him" and "Thank You and Goodnight," went to number twenty-five and forty-one, respectively; these songs were followed by a series of releases in 1964 and 1965 that did not make it onto the charts. The Angels' failure to come up with a second major hit may have been the fault of their producers. After producing "My Boyfriend's Back," Gottehrer, Feldman, and Goldstein had become involved in a variety of other projects, including numerous other girl groups as well as their own singing group (the Strangeloves, who broke into the Top Ten with "I Want Candy" in mid-1965), and the Angels eventually fell by the wayside.

selves with a hit single but then, unable to come up with a suitable follow-up, could not sustain their success. Among these groups were the Angels, who became the first white girl group to hit number one on the pop charts in the summer of 1963, when "My Boyfriend's Back" was released on Mercury's Smash label. That same year, the Jaynetts (Yvonne Bushnell, Ethel Davis, Ada Ray, and Mary Sue Wells) reached the number two position with a bizarre song entitled "Sally Go 'Round the Roses." While most of the popular girl groups were black, many of the girl groups who fell into the category of "one-hit wonders" were white. Recording on the Chattahoochee label, the Murmaids (Carol Fischer, Terry Fischer, and Sally Gordon) went to number three in December 1963 with "Popsicles and Icicles." A Brooklyn act known as Reparata and the Delrons (Sheila Reilly, Carol Drobnicki, and Mary Aiese) had a hit in the New York area with "Whenever a Teenager Cries," recorded on World Artists in 1964, but the song only made it to number sixty on the national charts.

In 1964 songwriters Jerry Leiber (1933–   ) and Mike Stoller (1933–   ), who had written numerous hits during the fifties for artists like Elvis Presley and the Coasters, formed the Red Bird label with the assistance of promoter George Goldner. With Jeff Barry and Ellie Greenwich as their primary songwriting and production team, Red Bird focused primarily on girl groups. The label's first release was a song called "Chapel of Love," written by Barry, Greenwich, and Phil Spector,

The Murmaids (seated, with unidentified woman at far right) with (standing, left to right) Stan Ross, owner of Gold Star Studios; Ruth Conti, president of Chattahoochee Records; and producer Kim Fowley.

and performed by a trio from New Orleans known as the Dixie Cups. The record went to number one, and was followed by another Barry-Greenwich composition called "People Say," which made it to number twelve. The Dixie Cups recorded several more songs for Red Bird, the most successful of which was a traditional New Orleans number called "Iko Iko," which reached number twenty. Thinking that the Dixie Cups would be better off working for a major label, the group's manager got them a deal with ABC Records. Unfortunately for the group, however, none of the records they made after leaving Red Bird managed to make the charts.

Barry and Greenwich also wrote for Red Bird artists such as the Butterflies, the Jelly Beans, and the Shangri-Las. The last group, consist-

Elvis Presley peruses the sheet music to "Jailhouse Rock," one of his many hits written by Mike Stoller (left) and Jerry Leiber (right).

Jeff Barry (1938–) and Ellie Greenwich (1940–)

Like Goffin and King, Jeff Barry and Ellie Greenwich became extremely successful during the sixties as a husband-and-wife songwriting team. After meeting at a Thanksgiving dinner at Greenwich's aunt's house, they began composing together and became romantically involved. Greenwich had learned to play piano while growing up on Long Island, and as a teenager in the late fifties she released a single on RCA under the name Ellie Gaye. In 1961 she began working as a songwriter at Trio Music for Jerry Leiber and Mike Stoller; in 1962 she married Barry. By the time he met Greenwich, Barry had written hundreds of songs, including a 1960 hit for Ray Peterson, "Tell Laura I Love Her." Together, Barry and Greenwich wrote classic pop tunes for a number of the girl groups, in addition to recording several songs in 1963 as the Raindrops, including "What a Guy," "The Kind of Boy You Can't Forget," and "Hanky Panky" (which became a number one hit in 1966 for Tommy James and the Shondells).

Barry and Greenwich produced and arranged many of their compositions, and although they initially shared production credits, Barry eventually persuaded Greenwich that his name should be the only one on the record so that he could build up his reputation in the industry. Barry reportedly argued to his wife that since she would eventually stop working and have children, she did not need to worry about her own career. When the couple split up, Greenwich found it difficult to work as a producer because of her lack of credentials.

The Dixie Cups

During the first half of 1964, the Dixie Cups were the only American group to have a number one single. Barbara Ann Hawkins (1943–), her sister Rosa Lee Hawkins (1944–), and Joan Marie Johnson (1945–) were discovered by a local artist named Joe Jones while singing in a New Orleans talent show in 1963. After becoming their manager, Jones brought the girls to New York to audition for Leiber and Stoller's Red Bird label. Originally the group was going to be called Little Miss and the Muffets, but at the last minute they were renamed the Dixie Cups. Songwriter Ellie Greenwich recalls the making of "Chapel of Love," their first hit: "After the session, I knew it was a number one record. 'Chapel of Love' and 'Leader of the Pack' [recorded by the Shangri-Las] were the only two I was dead sure about." Although Leiber and Stoller were credited with producing the record and received an additional percentage of the royalties as a result, Greenwich and her partner, Jeff Barry, were the true producers of this hit single.

Some girl groups, such as the Jelly Beans (above), included a male member singing backup vocals. According to composer Ellie Greenwich, who went to high school with George Morton (right) on Long Island, the eccentric producer-songwriter became known as "Shadow" because "he was never around and never could be found."

ing of four white teenage girls from Queens, became the most influential act on the Red Bird label. With help from producer-songwriter George "Shadow" Morton, Barry and Greenwich created a new sound for the Shangri-Las, producing melodramatic songs like "Remember (Walkin' in the Sand)" and their rebellious teen anthem "Leader of the Pack." Released in late 1964, "Leader of the Pack" quickly became a number one hit and the center of much controversy—it told the story of a girl's love for a young rebel who dies in a motorcycle crash. The song was banned in England, and some radio stations in the United States refused to play it as well. Nevertheless, the Shangri-Las were established as girl group stars, and they went on to have several more moderately suc-

The Shangri-Las

While many of the girl groups were similar in terms of their cute, schoolgirl look as well as their sound, the Shangri-Las projected a tough, hip image that stood out when they appeared in 1964. Sisters Mary and Betty Weiss and twins Marge and Mary Ann Ganser began singing together as students at Andrew Jackson High School in the New York City borough of Queens. In early 1964, they formed a group and signed a contract with Kama Sutra Productions, releasing a record that was soon forgotten on a small label called Spokane. At this point the Shangri-Las met George "Shadow" Morton, who became their producer and songwriter, as well as their manager. Morton got the girls a deal with Red Bird Records, and their first release on this label, "Remember (Walkin' in the Sand)," written by Morton, went to number five on the pop charts in 1964.

Morton also wrote the Shangri-Las' second single, "Leader of the Pack," which became the biggest hit of their career, spawning a Top Twenty parody entitled "Leader of the Laundromat" by the Detergents (with lead vocal by Ron Dante, who later sang on the Archies' 1969 hit "Sugar, Sugar"). The Shangri-Las were promptly catapulted into the spotlight, and they flew to England for a brief promotional tour. Lead singer Mary Weiss, who was only sixteen years old at the time, was unable to make the trip, and the group simply performed without her. The Shangri-Las often appeared as a trio in the United States as well, for Betty and Marge both left the group temporarily at different times. Like so many other girl groups, the Shangri-Las never received any royalties for their songs, partly as a result of the contract they had signed early in their career with Kama Sutra. Red Bird and "Shadow" Morton also took a portion of their earnings, and by the time the group had paid for studio costs, the money was gone. The group went on to make several more records for Red Bird, including one of the teenage soap operas that became their trademark, "Give Us Your Blessings," about a young couple who die in a car crash while trying to elope. Their last Top Ten hit was a heart-rending Morton composition, "I Can Never Go Home Anymore," in which a daughter's selfishness results in her mother's death.

cessful records on Red Bird, most of which were also written by Barry and Greenwich. By 1966 Red Bird had begun to disintegrate, and the Shangri-Las moved to Mercury Records. After releasing a few singles that failed to chart, they continued touring for several more years before fading into obscurity.

Phil Spector began his career in the music business as a member of the Teddy Bears (from left to right: Phil Spector, Annette Kleinbard, Marshall Leib). This group recorded their hit song "To Know Him Is To Love Him" in three hours at Gold Star Studios in Los Angeles.

The Tycoon of Teen

Although Phil Spector began his career in music as a performer, it was as a producer that he gained his reputation as a genius and became a legend in the rock and roll world. He created what came to be called the "wall of sound" by using a technique known as overdubbing, which involved recording music tracks on top of one another, as well as having several musicians play the same instruments at the same time to achieve a fuller, richer sound. After moving from Los Angeles to New York in 1960, Spector gained experience as a producer for several female artists, including Arlene Smith, who had been the lead singer for the Chantels. During this time, he also worked with Jerry Leiber and Mike Stoller as a studio musician, in addition to cowriting "Spanish Harlem" (with Leiber), the first solo record put out by Ben E. King (the former lead singer of the Drifters). In 1961 Spector produced a white trio called the Paris Sisters (Priscilla, Albeth, and Sherrell) singing "I Love How You Love Me," which went to number five on the charts and sold over a million copies.

By the end of 1961, Spector had joined with Lester Sill to establish Philles Records. One of the first groups he signed was the Crystals, who made their Philles debut with a Top Twenty record called "There's No Other (Like My Baby)" (1961), which was written by a friend of theirs named Leroy Bates and produced by Spector. Under Spector's guidance, the Crystals went on to hit the charts with a song originally intended for Tony Orlando called "Uptown," composed by husband-and-wife team

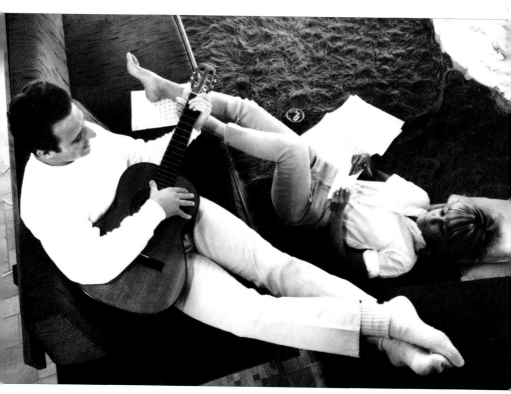

Barry Mann and his wife and songwriting partner, Cynthia Weil. Mann supposedly came up with the lyrics to the Paris Sisters' "I Love How You Love Me" in fifteen minutes.

Phil Spector (1940–)

One of the most talented producers in the history of rock and roll, Phil Spector was an eccentric genius who changed the face of popular music during the sixties. Born on December 26, 1940, in a Bronx neighborhood known as Soundview, Harvey Phillip Spector grew up in a lower-middle-class Jewish family. When Phil was eight years old, his father committed suicide. A few years later the family moved to West Hollywood, California, where Spector began playing guitar and writing songs. While still in high school, he composed "To Know Him Is To Love Him," the title of which was taken from the inscription on his father's tombstone. In 1958 he recorded the song for Dore Records with his group the Teddy Bears (consisting of Spector, Marshall Leib, and lead vocalist Annette Kleinbard, who later changed her name to Carol Connors and penned such hits as "Hey Little Cobra," performed by the Rip Chords, and "Gonna Fly Now [Theme from Rocky]"), and it became his first number one hit in any capacity—songwriter, producer, or performer.

Although the Teddy Bears' debut single sold more than a million copies, the group did not receive all the royalties that the label owed them, and they left Dore for Imperial Records, a larger independent label that had artists such as Fats Domino and Ricky Nelson. The Teddy Bears released an album and several singles on Imperial, but none of these recordings sold well, and the group split up in 1959. Meanwhile Spector, who was still a teenager, had gained a greater understanding of the music industry. When the Teddy Bears dissolved, he went to work for manager-promoter Lester Sill and his partner Lee Hazelwood, where he learned more about production techniques. Spector made a few recordings for Sill and Hazelwood's Trey label that were released under the name of the Spector's Three. While these records failed to make the charts, Lester Sill saw that Spector had great talent as a songwriter and producer. Sill had connections in New York with Jerry Leiber and Mike Stoller (he had, in fact, discovered them in the early fifties), and he got Phil a job working with them. For a while after Spector arrived in New York in 1960, he was sleeping on a couch in Leiber and Stoller's office. Within a few years, however, he had become the quintessential rock entrepreneur—a millionaire who controlled virtually every aspect of making and promoting his records.

Barry Mann and Cynthia Weil. (Mann had his own hit record with "Who Put the Bomp," a song he composed with Gerry Goffin, in 1961, and he and Weil wrote a number of other popular songs, such as the Drifters' "On Broadway.")

Despite these successes, the Crystals apparently did not enjoy working with Spector, and they hated the next song he made them record, a Goffin and King work entitled "He Hit Me (And It Felt Like a Kiss)." Spector's decision to release this song as a single might have been intended as an affront to his partners, who disliked the song as much as the

Crystals did. In any case, the song's masochistic content made it certain that it would provoke controversy. Spector went on to produce "He's a Rebel" (late 1962), a song written by Gene Pitney that went straight to number one, and "He's Sure the Boy I Love" (early 1963). Although these songs were released as Crystals records, the vocals were actually recorded

Although Phil Spector is just over five and a half feet (1.6m) tall, he was a giant in the pop music industry through the early sixties.

by a group of Los Angeles background singers known as the Blossoms, which included Fanita James, Gloria Jones, Jean King, and lead singer Darlene Love (born Darlene Wright in 1938). Because their name was legally owned by Philles Records, the real Crystals had no control over this substitution. When Phil decided to produce their next recording sessions in a Los Angeles studio and they were reluctant to make the trip on a plane, he simply replaced them. In spite of their disagreements with Spector, the Crystals went on to record two more hits with him, "Da Doo Ron Ron" and "Then He Kissed Me," both written by Ellie Greenwich and Jeff Barry.

In addition to regular appearances on the television show **Shindig,** *the Blossoms, led by Darlene Love (left), served as backup singers for Marvin Gaye and other artists in* **The T.A.M.I. (Teenage Awards Music International) Show.**

The Crystals

The Crystals were five Brooklyn schoolgirls who came together in 1961, shortly before they were signed by Phil Spector. Mary Thomas, Dee Dee Kennibrew, Dolores "La La" Brooks, Patricia Wright, and lead singer Barbara Alston started singing together just for fun. They began working with songwriter Leroy Bates and took their name from his daughter, Crystal. The Crystals had a raw R&B sound that appealed to Spector; the marketability of this sound—combined with the girls' youth and inexperience, which allowed Spector to mold them as he saw fit—enabled Spector to use the Crystals to establish his newly created Philles label. During their tenure with Spector, the Crystals were credited with six songs that made it into the Top Twenty. However, some of these songs, including the Crystals' biggest hit, "He's a Rebel," were actually recorded by Darlene Love and the Blossoms.

Spector had almost complete control over the Crystals' career—when he obtained full ownership of the Philles label, he used the group to fulfill a contractual obligation to his former partners by having them record a song that was never intended for release—"(Let's Dance) The Screw." By simply recording the song, Spector fulfilled the terms of his contract. He never released the song because he didn't want his partners to make any money from it. By the summer of 1963, Spector was focusing his attention on the Ronettes, and the Crystals were of little importance to him. The group was now a quartet—Mary Thomas had left and Pat Wright had been replaced by Frances Collins. In early 1964, the group toured England for the first time, backed up by the British band Manfred Mann. Realizing that Spector had lost interest in them, the Crystals sued him for royalties they had not received. While they were not awarded any money, they gained the right to continue using their name, and in 1965 the group signed a deal with United Artists Records. A year later, after releasing a few unsuccessful singles, the Crystals were dropped by the label and their recording career came to an end.

Murray "the K," a popular DJ on WINS New York in the early sixties, initially used the Ronettes as dancing girls between acts at the rock and roll revues he hosted on a regular basis.

Spector's next girl group was a trio named the Ronettes whom he had discovered performing with disc jockey Murray "the K" Kaufman (d. 1982) in New York. Phil fell in love with their lead singer, Veronica "Ronnie" Bennett, and became determined to make her a star. The Ronettes' first record, the Barry-Greenwich tune "Be My Baby," was released in August 1963. Recording engineer Larry Levine, who had been working with rock artists since the mid-fifties, recalls being in the studio with Spector when the Ronettes recorded this song: "[I]f something was remotely possible, he was gonna do it, and we just went ahead without second thought. There were no rock and roll rules for Phil, because he was making them up as he went along."

After the initial sessions with the Ronettes, Spector spent six weeks making a Christmas album that featured traditional carols performed with rock and roll arrangements. With performances by the Ronettes, the

Although Phil and the Ronettes (with Ronnie Spector at right) are shown here clowning around in the studio, Phil took actual recording sessions very seriously, forcing the singers and musicians to perform countless takes of a song until he felt it was right.

The Ronettes

Originally known as Ronnie and the Relatives, the Ronettes were a trio consisting of sisters Veronica (1943–) and Estelle Bennett (1944–) and their cousin Nedra Talley (1946–). These young women grew up in New York's Spanish Harlem and began singing together while they were teenagers. By 1961 they had signed a contract with Colpix Records, and during the next two years they released several singles that failed to chart. During this time, in addition to working as backup singers for Del Shannon and other artists, Ronnie and the Relatives were regular performers at one of New York's hottest nightclubs, the Peppermint Lounge, where they danced and sang with the house band, Joey Dee and the Starlighters. This engagement led to their appearances in music shows hosted by DJ Murray "the K" Kaufman at Brooklyn's Fox Theater.

The Ronettes were signed by Phil Spector in March 1963, after they got out of their contract with Colpix by telling the label that they were tired of the music business and wanted to go back to school. The group had already begun recording with Spector, and five months after they left Colpix, "Be My Baby" was released, reaching number two on the pop charts. Although the Ronettes went on to record a handful of other hits produced by Spector, their first single was their most successful. The group slowly disintegrated as Phil fell in love with Ronnie and began to separate her from the other Ronettes. Many of the songs they recorded during their years with Spector went unreleased because of Spector's fear of putting out a record that might not be a hit. During their last two years together, the Ronettes had only three songs that broke into the Top One Hundred, with the most popular reaching only as high as number fifty-two.

Crystals, Darlene Love, and a trio called Bob B. Soxx and the Blue Jeans (consisting of Darlene Love, Fanita James, and Bobby Sheen), *A Christmas Gift for You from Phil Spector* appeared in November. The album was produced with the same spectacular techniques Spector used on his pop records, but it did not sell well and was generally ignored by the listening public.

Spector's next effort was a follow-up single for the Ronettes. "Baby, I Love You," released in early 1964, made it as high as number twenty-four on the *Billboard* charts. By this time, Phil and Ronnie were romantically involved (although Phil was still married to his first wife, Annette Merar Spector). The Ronettes embarked upon a tour of England—where their records were very successful—appearing with the Rolling Stones, who had not yet become known in the United States. While in England with the Ronettes, Spector helped produce the Stones' "Not Fade Away," a song that had originally been recorded by Buddy Holly in the fifties and would become the Stones' first big hit in America.

Phil and Ronnie going over an arrangement of "Frosty the Snowman" for Phil's Christmas album, A Christmas Gift for You. *Phil thought this record would be hailed as a masterpiece, but it flopped when it was released.*

By the middle of 1964, the Philles label had ceased to be the hit factory it had been in the previous two years. Although Spector's output had not diminished, he was increasingly reluctant to release songs unless he was certain they would become smash hits. This cautiousness sometimes caused him to sit on a record that might have been a success, as in the case of the song "Chapel of Love," which he had recorded both with the Crystals and with the Ronettes. When Jeff Barry and Ellie Greenwich realized Spector was not going to release either version of the song, they produced yet another rendition with the Dixie Cups. "Chapel of Love" became that group's first number one record. As a result, Spector ended his working relationship with Barry and Greenwich, who had written a substantial number of hits for Philles.

When Barry and Greenwich recorded their song "All Grown Up" in the summer of 1964 with a group called the Exciters (Brenda Reid, Carol

The Exciters were originally an all-girl quartet known as the Masterettes, who sang in the company of a male group called the Masters. Eventually Herbert Rooney of the Masters joined the Masterettes, and the group was renamed the Exciters.

Johnson, Lillian Walker, and Herbert Rooney, who had a Top Ten hit with "Tell Him" in late 1962), Spector hurriedly released the Crystals' version of the song, which he had recorded with them a year earlier. Although the Crystals' rendition of "All Grown Up" barely made it onto the Top One Hundred, it effectively squelched the release of the Exciters' effort. Meanwhile the Ronettes (and Phil Spector) were back in the Top Forty with "(The Best Part of) Breakin' Up" and "Do I Love You." Their next single, "Walking in the Rain," composed by Spector, Barry Mann, and Cynthia Weil, reached number twenty-three. The Ronettes released a few more singles over the next two years, but none of these even came close to achieving the success of the group's earlier efforts. After accompanying the Beatles on their final tour of the United States, the group disbanded in late 1966.

Phil had become increasingly possessive of Ronnie toward the end of her career as a Ronette, and he refused to let her tour with them on several occasions (he could always find someone to take her place). Even before the Ronettes broke up, Spector had essentially given up on girl groups as a means for producing hit records. Early 1965 saw the release of the last number one record Spector would produce in the sixties, a passionate pop epic entitled "You've Lost That Lovin' Feelin'," written by Mann and Weil and sung by the Righteous Brothers (Bobby Hatfield and Bill Medley). This song, which was perhaps Spector's biggest success ever, was followed in 1966 by a recording of Tina Turner performing "River Deep, Mountain High" (written by Barry and Greenwich), which was a tremendous commercial failure. Unable to cope with this rejection, Spector withdrew from the music industry.

Phil Spector and Veronica Bennett were married in 1965, and Phil carried his all-powerful producer role into the husband-and-wife relationship; he made Ronnie a virtual prisoner in their home, forbidding her to leave the premises without his permission. In 1972, after years of

After breaking away from her husband and overcoming her alcoholism, Ronnie Spector was able to make a comeback. Here she is performing at the Bottom Line in New York City in 1987.

Even though he had, over the years, alienated many of his friends and colleagues in the music industry, Phil Spector received a lifetime achievement award from the Rock and Roll Hall of Fame in January 1989.

psychological abuse that led to a serious drinking problem, Ronnie escaped from Phil. Spector, who had become a millionaire in the mid-sixties at the age of twenty-four, emerged from his reclusive existence in the late sixties and early seventies to produce the Beatles' *Let It Be* album, as well as solo recordings by John Lennon and George Harrison, but he never regained his former status as the genius creator of classic pop masterpieces. In 1989 "The Tycoon of Teen," as Spector had been dubbed in a 1965 article by Tom Wolfe that appeared in the *New York Herald Tribune*, was inducted into the Rock and Roll Hall of Fame.

Although it eventually became one of the most successful black-owned businesses in the country, Motown Records was originally a shoestring operation based in a small house in Detroit, Michigan.

The Motown Sound

In the beginning, when someone said "the girls," it meant everyone. But past a certain point, when Berry referred to "the girls," he meant only the Supremes.

—Mary Wilson

While Phil Spector was producing hits with black groups like the Crystals and the Ronettes, a different kind of African-American pop sound was being created in Detroit, Michigan, as the founder of Motown Records, Berry Gordy, Jr., played a crucial role in the making of the Supremes and other girl groups that recorded for his label. In 1959 Gordy launched the Motown Record Corporation (whose name was derived from Detroit's nickname, "Motortown") and Tamla Records. In December 1961, Tamla had its first number one record on the pop and R&B charts with the

Berry Gordy (1929–   )

During the 1960s, the home of Motown Records was a two-story white frame house located at 2648 West Grand Boulevard in Detroit and distinguished by a large sign that read HITSVILLE, U.S.A. Berry Gordy, Jr., the man responsible for this musical empire, was a former lightweight boxer and Ford assembly-line worker who had owned a record store specializing in jazz in the early fifties. When the shop went bankrupt in 1955, Gordy turned to rhythm and blues for his next business venture. A few years later, he had become a successful songwriter, composing such songs as Jackie Wilson's Top Ten hit "Lonely Teardrops." By 1959 Gordy was interested in production and marketing as well as songwriting, and he was ready to start his own label.

Gordy founded the Tamla label that year, and its first release, Marv Johnson's "Come to Me," was leased to United Artists Records and reached number thirty on the pop charts. The first group signed by Tamla, a quintet called the Miracles, led by Smokey Robinson, recorded some singles that were leased to Chess Records. Motown began to distribute its own records in 1960 with the release of the Miracles' "Way Over There." When the group's follow-up, "Shop Around," hit the Top Ten in January 1961, Motown was on its way to becoming a serious contender in the music industry.

The idea behind Motown was to build a team of performers, songwriters, and producers who could manufacture a nonstop series of hits, much the same way that the assembly lines of Detroit's auto factories built cars. Gordy's strategy worked, resulting in mu-sic that appealed to both black and white audiences. As Jerry Wexler, who served as vice-president of Atlantic Records in the 1960s, put it, Motown accomplished "something that you would have to say on paper was impossible. They took black music and beamed it directly to the white American teenager." Although each of Motown's artists had a distinctly different sound, many of the label's records were similar to one another, featuring the trademark Motown Sound. This was partly a result of using the same group of studio musicians, collectively known as the Funk Brothers, who were usually paid a flat fee and received no credit for their work. The majority of Motown's releases featured a driving rhythm section laid down by this band, the core of which consisted of Earl Van Dyke on piano, James Jamerson on bass, and Benny Benjamin on drums. By 1966, the year that seventy-five percent of Motown's releases made the *Billboard* pop charts, Berry Gordy was the owner of the most successful independent label in the music business.

Marvelettes' "Please Mr. Postman." Their follow-up effort, "Twistin' Postman," made it only to number thirty-two, but they had better luck in 1962, breaking into the Top Ten with "Playboy." By 1963 their success had begun to evaporate, and they were starting to be outdone by other girl groups at Motown. While the Marvelettes did not achieve another Top Ten record until 1966, they continued to perform and record for the remainder of the decade.

Like Phil Spector, Berry Gordy was involved in almost every aspect of the music industry, and once he signed artists to his labels he took full control over their careers. When he founded Motown, Gordy also established a publishing company called Jobete Music and a management company called International Talent Management, Inc. All the songs written by Motown composers were published by Jobete, and all Motown artists were managed by International Talent; this gave Gordy a larger

Motown superstar Diana Ross hugs Berry Gordy at the reopening of New York's Apollo Theater in May 1985.

The Marvelettes

Motown's first girl group was formed in 1961 in the Detroit suburb of Inkster by a group of teenagers attending Inkster High School. Performing as the Marvels, Katherine Anderson (1944–), Georgeanna Dobbins (1944–1980), Wanda Young (1944–), Juanita Cowart (1944–), and Gladys Horton (1944–) entered a high school talent contest, competing for the opportunity to audition at Motown's Tamla label. They placed fourth in the contest, but their teacher, Mrs. Sharpley, was impressed enough to send them to Motown along with the top three acts. They sang several popular girl group songs, including the Chantels' "Maybe" and the Shirelles' "I Met Him on a Sunday," for Robert Bateman, who liked their sound but told them to produce some original material. They came up with "Please Mr. Postman," featuring lyrics written by Dobbins, and within a few weeks they recorded the song (with Marvin Gaye on drums). Berry Gordy changed the group's name to the Marvelettes, and "Please Mr. Postman" was released in the late summer of 1961. Fifteen weeks after entering the charts, it reached number one. The Marvelettes went on to have a few other Top Forty hits, including "Playboy" and "Beechwood 4-5789," but by 1963 Motown was busy promoting other groups. The Marvelettes regained some popularity in 1966 when Smokey Robinson wrote and produced their song "Don't Mess with Bill." Unfortunately for Motown's first girl group, however, by this time the Supremes had become the center of Gordy's attention, and the Marvelettes faded into the background.

Motown A&R department head William "Mickey" Stevenson (left), song-writer-producers Brian Holland (center) and Lamont Dozier (right), and singer-songwriter Smokey Robinson (seated) all composed hit tunes for Motown artists.

share of the profits and created a paternalistic relationship between him and his performers. Furthermore, according to music historians Joe McWeen and Jim Miller, International Talent served as "a kind of finishing school for Motown stars," teaching them the manners Gordy felt they would need in order to appeal to middle-class whites. Motown also had an extremely critical quality control division that carefully screened all releases before they were made available to the public.

Gordy had a great deal of input in the records that appeared on Motown, and under his direction the label quickly became an enormous success, living up to its slogan: THE SOUND OF YOUNG AMERICA. Employing a songwriting and production team commonly known as Holland-Dozier-Holland, which consisted of brothers Eddie and Brian Holland and Lamont Dozier, Motown developed a second popular female group, Martha and the Vandellas. Martha Reeves was working as a secretary for William "Mickey" Stevenson, head of the artists and repertoire (A&R) department at Motown, when she was hired as a backup singer for Marvin Gaye. In late 1962, she was signed by Motown's Gordy label as the lead vocalist of a trio named after Detroit's Van Dyke Avenue and Reeves's favorite singer, Della Reese. A year later, Martha and the Vandellas (as this new group was called) had their first Top Ten hit with "(Love Is Like a) Heat Wave," written and produced by Holland-Dozier-Holland.

The Supremes rehearse with songwriter-producers Holland-Dozier-Holland. Standing, from left to right: Diana Ross, Mary Wilson, Eddie Holland, Brian Holland. Seated: Lamont Dozier, Florence Ballard.

Toward the end of 1964, Martha and the Vandellas released their second million-seller, "Dancing in the Street." Cowritten by Mickey Stevenson and Marvin Gaye, the song became the group's biggest single, reaching the number two spot on the charts. Over the next three years, they made it into the Top Twenty with "Nowhere to Run," "I'm Ready for Love," "Jimmy Mack," and "Honey Chile," but their career languished as Berry Gordy poured his efforts into making another female group, the Supremes, into superstars. In 1967 Martha Reeves and the Vandellas (the

Martha and the Vandellas

When Martha Reeves auditioned as a singer for Motown Records in the early sixties, she was offered a job as a secretary. She had been singing with a group called the Del-Phis, who served as background vocalists for local artists and had recorded a single for Detroit's Check-Mate label, a subsidiary of Chicago's Chess Records. Working at Motown, even as a secretary, gave Reeves and the other Del-Phis—Rosalind Ashford, Annette Sterling, and lead singer Gloria Williams—an opportunity to provide backup vocals for various Motown artists. In 1962 Mary Wells missed a scheduled recording session, and the Del-Phis were called in to sing "There He Is (At My Door)," which was released on Motown's Melody label. Because of the group's contract with Check-Mate, they renamed themselves the Vels. When "There He Is" failed to make a significant showing on the charts, Williams left the group and Reeves took over as lead vocalist.

Reeves came up with a new name for the group—Martha and the Vandellas—and they were signed to Gordy Records, another subsidiary of Motown. Their next single, "I'll Have to Let Him Go," a song that had been rejected by Mary Wells, was another flop, but in 1963 they scored with "Come and Get These Memories," which went to number twenty-nine. This effort was the group's first collaboration with the songwriting-pro-duction team Holland-Dozier-Holland, who were also responsible for the group's follow-up record, "(Love Is Like a) Heat Wave." Released in the summer of 1963, "Heat Wave" became Martha and the Vandellas' first million-seller, propelling the group to stardom. At the end of the year, they had another hit with "Quicksand," which made it into the Top Ten, and Betty Kelly replaced Annette Sterling, who left the group to get married.

In 1964 Martha and the Vandellas recorded "Live Wire," "In My Lonely Room," and their biggest record, "Dancing in the Street," which was originally meant for Kim Weston, a solo artist at Motown. Martha and the Vandellas returned to the Top Ten in the spring of 1965 with "Nowhere to Run," another Holland-Dozier-Holland composition. Despite their success, the group was not entirely satisfied with the situation at Motown. And, as noted by historians Adam White and Fred Bronson, by this time "the Supremes were hogging the headlines, the top of the charts, and the attention of Holland-Dozier-Holland." "Jimmy Mack," a song the group recorded in mid-1964, was not released until 1967, most likely because of its resemblance to records made by the Supremes. Other releases, such as "I'm Ready for Love" (a Top Ten hit in 1966), were songs that had been rejected by the Supremes. Martha and the Vandellas were clearly no longer a priority at Motown, and "Honey Chile," which went to number eleven in 1967, was the group's last big hit. In 1968 Betty Kelly was replaced by Reeves's younger sister Lois, who had been a member of the Orlons, and in 1970 Rosalind Ashford was replaced by Sandra Tilley, who had been with the Velvelettes, another Motown group. Martha Reeves and the Vandellas continued performing and recording until 1971, when the group broke up, and Reeves left the Motown label in 1972.

group's name was amended that year, echoing the names of other Motown acts such as Smokey Robinson and the Miracles) had their last Top Forty hit, and in 1971 the group finally disbanded.

Although the girl group sound had largely disappeared from the charts by 1965, Motown became an exception to the rule, scoring hits with its girl groups into the late sixties. This was partly a result of the style of most of Motown's female artists, whose records consisted of slick, commercial material that appealed to a broader audience than the records produced by the girl groups of the early sixties. The Supremes came to exemplify this polished sound that in some ways bore more resemblance to the styles of white vocal groups of the fifties than those of girl groups like the Shirelles or the Chiffons. By the end of the decade, the Supremes had amassed a total of twelve number one singles (more than any other artist except the Beatles and Elvis Presley), making them the most successful and best known of all the girl groups.

The Supremes were signed to Motown at the beginning of 1961, making them the label's first female group. Despite the failure of their first two releases on the Tamla label—"I Want a Guy" and "Buttered Popcorn"—the group's ladylike image made an

A publicity photograph of the Primettes (the group that eventually became the Supremes) taken in 1961.

In later years, the Supremes abandoned their little-girl image in favor of a more glamorous look. Left to right: Diana Ross, Mary Wilson, and Florence Ballard.

impression on Gordy, and he committed himself to nurturing their career. Prior to their recording debut, the members of the group had taken turns singing the lead vocal. Gordy, however, made the decision that Diana Ross should be the lead singer of the Supremes, and he was reluctant to promote "Buttered Popcorn" because it featured Florence Ballard singing lead. This marked the beginning of tensions within the group, caused primarily by disagreements between Ross and Ballard that were often mediated by Mary Wilson, that would plague them throughout their career.

In January 1964, after switching from Tamla Records to the Motown label, the Supremes had their first entry in the Top Forty with a Holland-Dozier-Holland song entitled "When the Lovelight Starts Shining Through His Eyes." The song made it only as high as number twenty-three, but by working with Holland-Dozier-Holland the group stumbled upon the combination that would lead to a string of number one hits, the first of which was released in July 1964. "Where Did Our Love Go?" had originally been offered to the Marvelettes, who turned it down only to have the Supremes take the song to the top of the charts. By this point Diana Ross had perfected a vocal style that Alan Betrock, author of *Girl Groups: The Story of a Sound*, describes as "a stable mix of cutesy-poo delivery and highly articulated diction with histrionic theatricality."

By the end of 1964, the Supremes had taken two more songs—"Baby Love" and "Come See About Me"—to number one. They were filmed performing their hits for a documentary called *The T.A.M.I. Show* (T.A.M.I. was an acronym for Teenage Awards Music International), which featured British and American rock acts such as the Beach Boys, Gerry and the Pacemakers, Chuck Berry, Marvin Gaye, James Brown, Lesley Gore, and the Rolling Stones. When "Baby Love" went to number one in England for two weeks, the Supremes became the first girl group to reach the top of the British charts. In December they made their first appearance on *The Ed Sullivan Show*, which had generally shunned black girl groups in the early sixties. Over the next six months, the group scored again with "Stop! In the Name of Love" and

The Supremes

During the early sixties, Florence "Flo" Ballard (1943–1976), Diana (originally Diane) Ross (1944–), and Mary Wilson (1944–) were sometimes referred to at Motown as "the no-hit Supremes," for they released a string of records that flopped before "Where Did Our Love Go?" became their first number one single in 1964. The Supremes started out in 1959 as the female counterpart of a Detroit group called the Primes,

some of whom went on to form the Temptations. Known as the Primettes, the group consisted of Ballard, Ross, and Wilson, who had grown up together in the Brewster housing projects, and Betty Travis (later replaced by Barbara Martin). The Primettes began performing locally, and in 1960, after an unsuccessful auditon at Motown, they were signed by the small Lu-Pine label.

The songs they recorded for Lu-Pine were never released, and the Primettes started hanging around the Motown offices, where they were soon being used as background singers on various artists' studio sessions. After a second audition with Berry Gordy, the Primettes were signed to his Tamla label. At Gordy's request, Flo Ballard chose a new name for the group: the Supremes. At the time, Ross and Wilson were extremely unhappy with this choice, for they felt it sounded too masculine (and, in fact, an all-male group did use the name in the early sixties, though they later added a female vocalist and renamed themselves Ruby and the Romantics). Toward the end of 1961 Barbara Martin left the group and the Supremes became a trio. After releasing two singles that went unnoticed, the Supremes made their debut on the charts with "Your Heart Belongs to Me," which reached number ninety-five in August 1962.

Although many people seem to agree that Diana Ross did not necessarily have the best voice in the group, she was undoubtedly the most aggressive member of the Supremes. Her determination and Berry Gordy's favoritism eventually resulted in her being placed at the helm of the group. After she started working with Holland-Dozier-Holland in 1964, Ross began to develop a style that would lead the Supremes to one success after another. "Where Did Our Love Go?" established a pattern of carefully crafted pop material that was markedly different from the soulful songs produced by other Motown groups, such as Martha and the Vandellas. In spite of the group's initial objection to what Mary Wilson called "kiddy-bop stuff," it was this type of music that eventually turned the Supremes into international pop icons. In 1988 the Supremes became the first female group to be inducted into the Rock and Roll Hall of Fame.

While most of the girl groups received little attention from the media, the Supremes were known and loved across the United States. From left to right: Mary Wilson, Diana Ross, and Florence Ballard in a publicity photograph taken in 1966.

"Back in My Arms Again." The Supremes continued to rack up hit records in 1965 and 1966, with "I Hear a Symphony," "You Can't Hurry Love," and "You Keep Me Hangin' On."

While not all of the Supremes' releases went to the top of the charts, until 1967 all but one of their songs made it into the Top Ten. The Supremes were superstars, with their faces on the covers of *Time*, *Ebony*, and other well-known magazines. They appeared in commercials for such products as Coca-Cola and Arrid Deodorant, and they promoted their own brand of white bread. They performed at prestigious nightclubs across the country, including the Flamingo Hotel in Las Vegas and the Copacabana in New York. But in spite of their tremendous success, the

Supremes were not happy. As the lead singer and Berry Gordy's favorite, Diana Ross received most of the attention. The other Supremes resented this, and Florence Ballard began to express her dissatisfaction by being late to rehearsals and interviews and drinking excessively.

After Ballard missed several performances, she was forced to leave the group, and Cindy Birdsong (a former member of the group Patti LaBelle and the Bluebelles) became her replacement. At the same time, Gordy renamed the group Diana Ross and the Supremes. In 1968 Holland-Dozier-Holland ceased working with the Supremes, eventually breaking away from Motown to set up their own record labels, Invictus and Hot Wax. In December 1969 Motown released the last number one song by Diana Ross and the Supremes, "Someday We'll Be Together"; at the same time, Ross announced she was leaving the group to pursue a solo career. Although the Supremes were given credit for "Someday We'll Be Together," this song was actually Diana's first solo venture; Mary Wilson and Cindy Birdsong did not take part in the recording session (backing vocalists Maxine and Julia Waters sang what would have been their parts). After Ross departed from the Supremes, they found a replacement and continued as a group into the mid-1970s. In 1976, after experiencing a series of financial difficulties that left her dependent on welfare, Florence Ballard died of a heart attack at the age of thirty-two.

Say Goodbye to Girl Groups

While the end of the girl group era is difficult to pinpoint exactly, the trend began to lose its momentum in the mid-sixties, particularly after the so-called British Invasion, spearheaded by the arrival (and wild popularity) of the Beatles, took place. Other new sounds, such as folk-rock,

Peter Noone, lead singer of Herman's Hermits, learned "I'm Into Something Good" by listening to a copy of Carole King's demo tape.

surf music, and Southern soul produced by the Stax and Volt record labels, may also have contributed to the demise of the girl groups. By the mid-sixties, record companies were finding more groups that played and wrote their own material, and many producers and songwriters gave up trying to achieve hits with girl groups, feeling that they could not compete with these new, self-made artists. Trends in pop music usually tend to fade after a few years, and by 1965 the girl groups' control of the charts had for the most part run its course.

While the girl groups were beginning to disappear, the music they created continued to be popular with other recording artists and with the record-buying public. The cover songs that appeared on early Beatles albums, which included tunes that had been hits for the Shirelles, the Cookies, and the Marvelettes, demonstrate the Fab Four's fondness for the vocal harmonies used by R&B artists. Some girl groups were actually outdone by British groups that rerecorded their songs from a male perspective. Earl-Jean, lead singer of the Cookies, released her version of Goffin and King's "I'm Into Something Good" in 1964, only to be upstaged a few months later by an unknown band called Herman's Hermits, who took the song to number thirteen. The Exciters recorded a Barry-Greenwich composition called "Do Wah Diddy," which reached only as high as number seventy-eight; Manfred Mann's rendition, entitled "Do Wah Diddy Diddy," went all the way to number one.

Many years later, girl groups were still influencing male artists. In the late seventies, an eighteen-year-old actor named Shaun Cassidy (1958–   ) recorded two of Phil Spector's girl group masterpieces, "Be My Baby" and "Da Doo Ron Ron," on his debut album. The latter song, which was the first record Cassidy ever purchased, reached number one in July 1977 and helped to make its singer a teen idol. In 1980 the hard

rock supergroup Aerosmith had a minor hit with the Shangri-Las' "Remember (Walking in the Sand)." In 1982 "You Can't Hurry Love," a Supremes song, became a million-seller for British performer Phil Collins. That same year, a version of Martha and the Vandellas' "Dancing in the Street" was a minor hit for the rock group Van Halen; the song was also recorded in 1985 by Mick Jagger and David Bowie. Other performers have written new songs that clearly imitate the girl group sound, such as Billy Joel's 1981 hit "Say Goodbye to Hollywood," which Ronnie Spector recorded in 1977.

Shaun Cassidy introduced a whole new generation of listeners to songs originally popularized by the girl groups of the 1960s.

Girl Groups in the 1990s

While most female vocal groups of the nineties appear to have very little in common with the girl groups of the sixties, some similarities do exist between the female artists of these two eras. The best example is the group En Vogue, which was created by Denzil Foster and Thomas McElroy, two members of a band called Club Nouveau. Wanting to apply their songwriting and production skills to a female group, Foster and McElroy held auditions; they came up with a quartet consisting of Maxine Jones, Dawn Robinson, Cindy Herron, and Terry Ellis. These women spent a year living together and singing background vocals on various projects for their producers before they began recording as En Vogue.

Soon after their first album, *Born 2 Sing*, appeared in 1990, the group was labeled "the Supremes of the 1990s." Although some aspects of their career strongly resemble the careers of the Supremes and other sixties girl groups, En Vogue has more control over their work than most of their predecessors had. As one member of the group stated, "We think about what we want to sing about, and that's important to us." Foster and McElroy set out to promote a group that would appeal to women as well as men, and they realized that to achieve this aim the group had to be more than just talented sex symbols. Despite the fact that most of their music is written and produced by men, En Vogue projects an image of female independence, as expressed through such songs as "Free Your Mind" (from their album *Funky Divas*), which directly attacks sexist and racist attitudes.

The success of artists such as En Vogue illustrates that the music industry's attitude toward female artists has changed greatly over the past three decades. While sexism is undoubtedly still present in the world of popular music, women are taken more seriously as performers, and they

En Vogue often uses vocal harmonies and arrangements that resemble those used by the girl groups of the sixties in conjunction with modern styles of pop music.

have a much better chance of receiving the credit they deserve for their artistic contributions. The girl group era was not a particular triumph for feminism, but it did help to establish the fact that women could be successful pop singers, increasing the possibilities for future female artists. Most of the women who made up the girl groups discussed in this book are no longer involved in the music business, but in a relatively brief period of time they nevertheless managed to make a contribution to pop music and American pop culture that will last for years to come.

Bibliography

Bronson, Fred. *The Billboard Book of Number One Hits*. New York: Billboard Publications, 1988.

Curtis, Jim. *Rock Eras: Interpretations of Music and Society, 1954–1984*. Bowling Green, Ohio: Bowling Green State University Popular Press, 1987.

Fong-Torres, Ben, and Dave Marsh. *The Motown Album: The Sound of Young America*. New York: St. Martin's Press, 1990.

Hirshey, Gerri. *Nowhere to Run: The Story of Soul Music*. New York: Viking Penguin, 1984.

Lazell, Barry, ed. *Rock Movers and Shakers*. New York: Billboard Publications, 1989.

Miller, Jim, ed. *The Rolling Stone Illustrated History of Rock and Roll*. New York: Random House/Rolling Stone Press, 1980.

Nite, Norm N. *Rock On Almanac: The First Four Decades of Rock 'n' Roll*. New York: Harper & Row, 1989.

Pavletich, Aida. *Rock-a-Bye, Baby*. New York: Doubleday, 1980.

Ribowsky, Mark. *He's a Rebel*. New York: E.P. Dutton, 1989.

Stokes, Geoffrey, Ken Tucker, and Ed Ward. *Rock of Ages: The Rolling Stone History of Rock and Roll*. New York: Summit Books/Rolling Stone Press, 1986.

White, Adam, and Fred Bronson. *The Billboard Book of Number One Rhythm and Blues Hits*. New York: Billboard Publications, 1993.

Suggested Reading

Betrock, Alan. *Girl Groups: The Story of a Sound*. New York: Delilah Books, 1982.

Gaar, Gillian G. *She's a Rebel: The History of Women in Rock & Roll*. Seattle: Seal Press, 1992.

Spector, Ronnie, with Vince Waldron. *Be My Baby*. New York: Harmony Books, 1990.

Wilson, Mary, with Patricia Romanowski and Ahrgus Juilliard. *Dreamgirl: My Life as a Supreme*. New York: St. Martin's Press, 1986.

Suggested Listening

The Cookies. *The Complete Cookies*. Sequel Records.

Martha Reeves and the Vandellas. *Motown Legends*. Motown Records.

The Marvelettes. *Greatest Hits*. Motown Records.

The McGuire Sisters. *Greatest Hits*. MCA Records.

The Shirelles. *Anthology (1959–1965)*. Rhino Records.

Spector, Phil. *Back to Mono (1958–1969)*. Abkco Records.

The Supremes. *Greatest Hits*, Vols. 1 and 2. Motown Records.

Various Artists. *The Best of the Girl Groups*, Vols. 1 and 2. Rhino Records.

Photography Credits

Index

Aerosmith, 67
"All Grown Up," 48, 49
Andrews Sisters, 14, *14*
Angels, 30, *30*
Archies, 37
"Are You Still My Baby?," 25

"Baby, I Love You," 47
"Baby It's You," 25
"Baby Love," 62
Bacharach, Burt, 25
"Back in My Arms Again," 64
Ballard, Florence, 57, *57*, 61, *61, 62*, 63, *64*, 65
Barrett, Richard, 19, 20
Barry, Jeff, 31, 32, 33, *33*, 35, 37, 42, 44, 48, 50, 67
Beach Boys, 62
Beatles, 26, 29, 50, 51, 60, 65, 66
"Beechwood 4–5789," 55
"Bei Mir Bist Du Schon," 14
"Be My Baby," 44, 46, 67
Berry, Chuck, 62
Birdsong, Cindy, 65
Blossoms, 42, *42*
Bobbettes, *8*, 19
"Born Too Late," 17
Bowie, David, 67
Brown, James, 62
"Buttered Popcorn," 60, 61
Butterflies, 32
By Request, 17

Cassidy, Shaun, 67, *67*
"Chains," 26
Chantels, 19, 20, *20–21*, 21, 38, 55
"Chapel of Love," 31, 34, 48
"Charlie Brown," 18
Chiffons, 24, 28, 29, *29*, 60
Chordettes, 16–18, *18*
Chords, *11*, 12, 13
A Christmas Gift for You From Phil Spector, 47
Clovers, 20
Coasters, 18, 31
Collins, Phil, 67
"Come to Me," 53
Cookies, 26–27, *26–27*, 66
Crew Cuts, *12*, 13
Crossovers, 13
Crystals, 25, 39–43, *43*, 48, 52

"Da Doo Ron Ron," 67
"Dancing in the Street," 58, 59, 67
David, Hal, 25
DeCastro Sisters, 14, *15*
"Dedicated to the One I Love," 24
DeJohn Sisters, 14, *16*
Dion and the Belmonts, 27
Dixie Cups, 32, 34, *34*, 48
Dixon, Luther, 22, 24, 25
"Do I Love You," 49
"Don't Mess with Bill," 55
"Don't Say Nothin' Bad About My Baby," 26
Doo-wop, 11, 19
"Do Wah Diddy," 67
Dozier, Lamont, *56*, 57, *57*, 59, 62, 63, 65
Drifters, 23, 39, 40

"Eddie My Love," 18
En Vogue, 68–69, *69*
"Every Night (I Pray)," 20
Exciters, 48–49, *49*, 67

Fontane Sisters, 14, 18
"Foolish Little Girl," 22, 25
Four Aces, 17
Four Pennies, 29
Frankie Lymon and the Teenagers, 19
Franklin, Aretha, 23

Gaar, Gillian, 9
Gaye, Marvin, 55, 57, 58, 62
Gerry and the Pacemakers, 62
"Give Us Your Blessings," 37
Goffin, Gerry, 22, 23, *23*, 26, 27, 28, *28*, 40, 66
"Goodnight, Sweetheart, Goodnight," 14–15
Gordy, Berry, Jr., 52, 53, *53*, 54, *54*, 55, 56, 58, 61, 63, 65
Gore, Lesley, 62
Greenberg, Florence, 25
Greenwich, Ellie, 31, 32, 33, *33*, 34, 35, 37, 42, 44, 48, 50, 67

"Hanky Panky," 33
Harlem Queens, 19
Harrison, George, 29, 51
Herman's Hermits, 23, 66–67, *66*
"He's a Rebel," 25, 41, 43
"He's Gone," 20
"He's So Fine," 27–28, 29
Holland, Brian, *56*, 57, *57*, 59, 61, 62, 63, 65
Holland, Eddie, 57, *57*, 59, 61, 62, 63, 65
Holly, Buddy, 47

"I Adore Him," 30
"I Can Never Go Home Anymore," 37
"I Feel the Earth Move," 23
"I Hear a Symphony," 64
"Iko Iko," 32
"I Love How You Love Me," 39
"I Love You So," 20
"I Met Him on a Sunday," 24, 55
"I'm Into Something Good," 23, 27, 66
"I'm Not a Juvenile Delinquent," 19
"I'm Ready for Love," 58, 59
"In My Lonely Room," 59
"I Shot Mr. Lee," 19
"It Might As Well Rain Until September," 23
"It's Too Late," 23
"It's Unbearable," 27
"I Want a Guy," 60
"I Want Candy," 30

James, Tommy, 33
Jaynetts, 30
Jelly Beans, 32, 35, *35*
"Jimmy Mack," 58, 59
Joel, Billy, 67
Joey Dee and the Starlighters, 46
Johnson, Marv, 53

Kaufman, Murray "the K," 44, *44*, 46
"The Kind of Boy You Can't Forget," 33
King, Ben E., 39
King, Carole, 22, 23, *23*, 24, 26, 27, 28, *28*, 40, 66
Kirshner, Don, 23, *28*

My Boyfriend's Back!

LaBelle, Patti, 65
"Leader of the Pack," 34, 35
Leiber, Jerry, 31, 32, 33, 34, 38, 39, 40
Lennon, John, 51
Lennon Sisters, 14
"The Lion Sleeps Tonight," 29
Little Eva, 23, 26, 28, 28
"Live Wire," 59
"The Loco-Motion," 23, 26, 28
"Lollipop," 17, 18
"Lonely Teardrops," 53
"Look in My Eyes," 20
Love, Darlene, 42, 43, 43, 47
"Love, Love, Love," 20
"(Love Is Like a) Heat Wave," 57, 59

"Mama Said," 24
Mann, Barry, 39, 40, 49, 50
Marcus, Greil, 8
Martha and the Vandellas, 57, 58, 59, 63, 67
Marvelettes, 54, 55, 55, 62, 66
"Maybe," 19, 20
McGuire Sisters, 14–16, 17
Miracles, 53, 60
Moonglows, 15
Morton, George "Shadow," 35, 35, 37
Motown sound, 52–65
"Mr. Lee," 19
"Mr. Sandman," 17, 18
Murmaids, 30, 31
"My Boyfriend's Back," 30
"My Sweet Lord," 29

"Never on Sunday," 18
Nevins, Al, 23, 28
"Nobody Knows What's Goin' On (In My
    Mind But Me)," 29
"Not Fade Away," 47
"Nowhere to Run," 58, 59

"On Broadway," 40
"One Fine Day," 28

Paris Sisters, 39
"People Say," 32
Peterson, Ray, 33
Pitney, Gene, 25, 41
"Playboy," 54, 55
"The Plea," 20
"Please, Mr. Postman," 54, 55
Poni-Tails, 7, 17
"Popsicles and Icicles," 30–31
Presley, Elvis, 31, 32, 60
Primettes, 60, 60

"Quicksand," 59

Racism, 9, 68
Raindrops, 33
Reeves, Martha, 57, 58, 59
"Remember (Walkin' in the Sand)," 35, 37,
    67
Reparata and the Delrons, 31
Rhythm and blues, 6, 8, 11, 13, 14, 16, 18,
    19, 20, 24, 29, 43, 52, 53, 66
Righteous Brothers, 50
"River Deep, Mountain High," 50
Robinson, Smokey, 53, 55, 56, 60
Rockabilly, 11
Rock and roll, 7, 11, 13
Rock and Roll Hall of Fame, 51, 63
Rolling Stones, 29, 47, 62, 67
Ronald and Ruby, 18

Ronettes, 44–50, 45, 46, 47
Ross, Diana, 53, 53, 57, 57, 61, 61, 62, 62,
    63, 64, 65
Ruby and the Romantics, 63

"Sally Go 'Round the Roses," 30
Shangri-Las, 32, 34, 35, 36–37, 36–37, 67
"Sh-Boom," 11, 12, 13
Shepherd Sisters, 14
She's A Rebel (Gaar), 9
Shirelles, 22, 24–25, 24–25, 29, 55, 60, 66
Shondells, 33
"Shop Around," 53
"Sincerely," 15
"Soldier Boy," 22, 25
"Someday We'll Be Together," 65
Spaniels, 15
"Spanish Harlem," 39
Spector, Phil, 31, 38–42, 38, 44–51, 45,
    52, 67
Stevenson, William "Mickey," 56, 57, 58
Stoller, Mike, 31, 32, 33, 34, 38, 40
"Stop! In the Name of Love," 62
Strangeloves, 30
"Sugar, Sugar," 37
Supremes, 52, 55, 57, 57, 58, 58, 59,
    60–65, 61, 63, 64, 67
"Sweet Talkin' Guy," 28, 29

"Take Good Care of My Baby," 23
Tapestry, 23
Teddy Bears, 38, 40
"Tell Him," 49
"Tell Laura I Love Her," 33
Temptations, 63
"Thank You and Goodnight," 30
"Then He Kissed Me," 42
"There's No Other (Like My Baby)," 39
Tokens, 29
"To Know Him Is To Love Him," 38, 40
"Tonight's the Night," 24, 29
Turner, Big Joe, 8
Turner, Tina, 50

"Up on the Roof," 23

Valentines, 20
Vee, Bobby, 23

"Walking in the Rain," 49
Warwick, Dionne, 25
"Way Over There," 53
Weil, Cynthia, 39, 40, 49, 50
"Well, I Told You," 20
Wells, Mary, 59
"What A Guy," 33
"Whenever a Teenager Cries," 31
"When the Lovelight Starts Shining Through
    His Eyes," 61
"Where Did Our Love Go?," 62, 63
"Who Put the Bomp," 40
"Why Do Fools Fall in Love," 19
"Will You Love Me Tomorrow?," 22, 24
Wilson, Jackie, 53
Wilson, Mary, 52, 57, 57, 61, 61, 62, 63,
    64, 65

"You Can't Hurry Love," 64, 67
"You Keep Me Hangin' On," 64
"You Make Me Feel Like A Natural
    Woman," 23
"Your Heart Belongs to Me," 63
"You've Lost That Lovin' Feelin'," 50